Decorating with Dried Flowers

Decorating with Dried Flowers

Deborah Miles

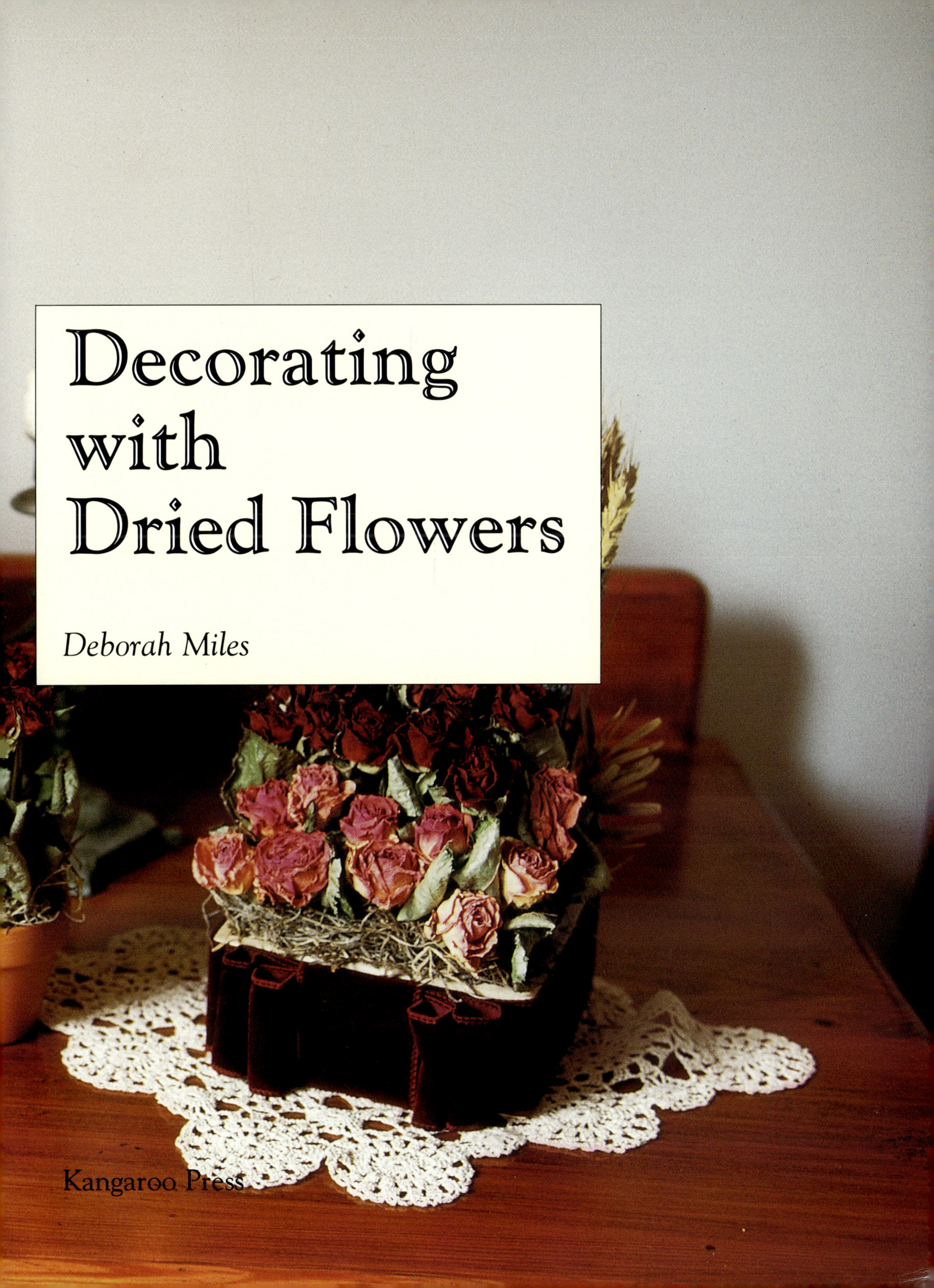

Kangaroo Press

Acknowledgments
My thanks to:

- My husband Colin and son Shane, who are often left to their own devices when the creative urge takes hold.
- My mother Alicia for her belief, support and love.

Photography
B. & G. Williamson, Bomaderry NSW
R. Miller, Berry, NSW (pages 7, 9, 35, 36)
Deborah Miles (pages 12, 18, 24, 30)

First published in 1996 by Kangaroo Press Pty Ltd
3 Whitehall Road, Kenthurst NSW 2056 Australia
PO Box 6125 Dural Delivery Centre NSW 2158
Printed in Hong Kong through Colorcraft Ltd

ISBN 0 86417 759 3

Contents

DRIED

Introduction

Decorating with dried flowers has become increasingly popular as people realise the lasting beauty they bring into the home. The simplest arrangement creates a homey atmosphere, especially when it is stamped with your own personal touch.

Being creative means being able to see the potential in objects both regular and unusual, and to have decorative ideas spring to mind. Not all ideas work, but experimenting leads to more ideas being generated.

'Where do you get all your ideas?' is a question I am often asked. I can't really say—I might be looking at a magazine or gazing out the car window when an idea comes to mind. I do, however, often find inspiration at times when I wish to create something special, in people's gardens.

There are no hidden secrets to the works I am presenting in this book. Creativity, to my mind, is having the confidence to try something new or different. At times we may need a guiding hand to help us on our way. This is what I hope this book will provide. Books currently available provide an abundance of information on how to dry flowers, which I do not wish to replicate. What I am presenting here is a variety of decorating ideas using pots, boxes, photo frames, wooden frames and mirrors, ideas with a difference.

Other questions I am regularly asked are: 'Do you teach classes?', 'How do you make this?' and 'How do you find the time?'—but none of the works presented in this book is difficult or time consuming and all can be done a section at a time (one of the great benefits of working with dried material).

OPPOSITE: Bunches of dried hydrangea add life to an interesting collection of old bits and pieces

Decorated bookends are an ideal way to display your favourite books

You can change the whole character of any of these floral decorations simply by changing the ribbon or the flowers. You can use the basic ideas presented here as a jumping-off point to create works that are stamped with your own individuality. If you do this then I have succeeded in my aim.

I build my own frames to suit the works I wish to create. I tend to favour oregon and aged Baltic pine from recycling yards. Frames and boards can be made quite cheaply using pine tongue-and-groove from hardware stores, or old fence palings. Craft supply shops have pre-cut folk art templates that can be used to great effect as well.

There are no hidden secrets to creating works with stunning effect. Nothing is more satisfying than when your dried flower creation is complimented and you can say, 'I made it myself.'

A decorated and recycled Welcome sign can give visitors a friendly country greeting

Materials

Floral Oasis
Flowers (both dried and artificial)
Leaves, seedpods and grains
Artificial fruit
Craft glue/glue gun
Liquid nails
Scissors
Florist's wire
Variety of pots and other containers
Pliers
Eye-hooks or screws
Picture-hanging wire
Boards

If you are going to make your own frames you will need wood, a saw, mitre box, wood glue, tape measure, 90° and 45° square rule, sandpaper, nails and a hammer. See page 37 for instructions for making frames.

To keep your costs down, consider having a 'creating day' with a group of friends.

Displaying your arrangements

How and where you display your finished arrangements can make a world of difference to their overall appearance and to that of the room. Some arrangements may look good as a focal piece, while others may show to more advantage combined with pictures or books. Some may look better positioned near a window, or on a mantelpiece or table with a group of ornaments.

Try moving your arrangement to different positions until you find the spot where it has maximum effect. Most arrangements will look good in one spot and not another.

Collections of work with a common colour theme clustered together are pleasing to the eye and can create a formal and elegant look.

The same applies to a collection of plates on a wall or sideboard. Add a wreath or other arrangement with a similar theme for an informal country-style look.

Flower-filled photo frames take on a whole new look when they are displayed on the wall with a collection of your family photos.

A collection of arrangements with a common theme can create a formal and elegant look

Natives in half pots

Materials
prepared board (see page 37 for instructions)
half pot or pots
glue gun and glue stick or craft glue
Oasis
scissors
wheat
oats
rice
hops
formosa
proteas, waratahs, dryandra
poppy pods
straw flowers or flannel flowers
banksia flowers and pods
tetragona pods
raffia
(Optional: 3 cm pot, almonds, wire)

These flowers are suggested only as a guide. If you are not able to obtain any of them, substitute something else (and yes, I realise that proteas, poppy pods and grains aren't natives). Some of the flowers and pods I collected from my own garden and dried just by hanging them in the kitchen.

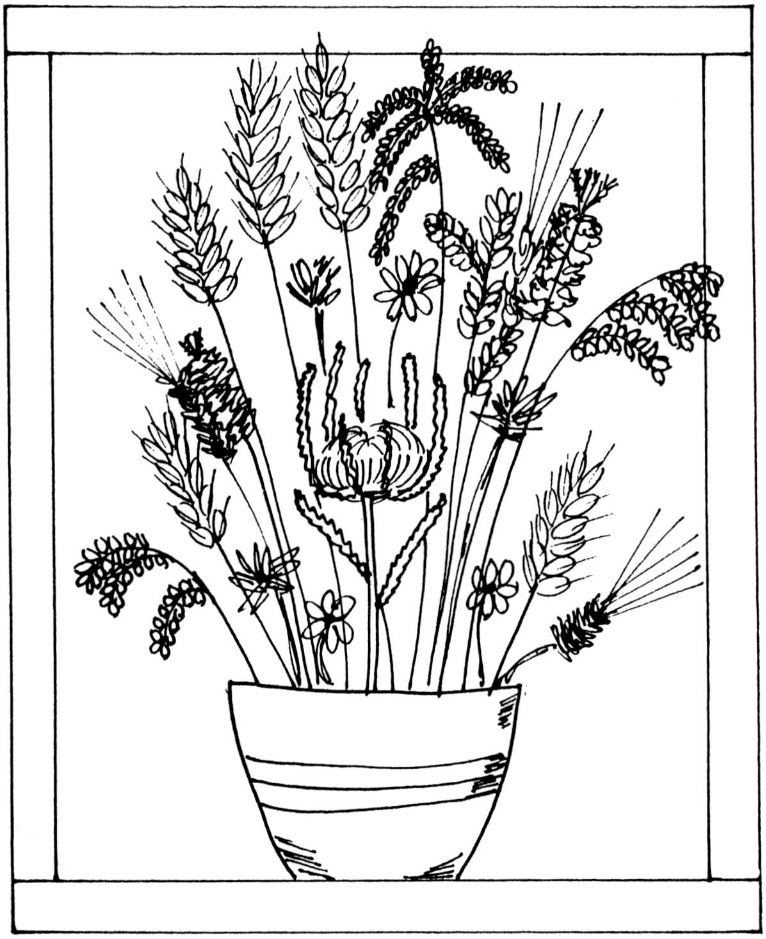

Opposite and Left: Arrangements extending into the frame help to soften the outline

Half pots grouped on a board. Ribbons can be used to link an arrangement to an existing colour scheme

Glue the pot or pots to the board (see page 37). Cut the Oasis to fit and glue inside each pot. Working from the back of the pot, start by cutting wheat and oats to a length where their tips come just above board height, and push them into the Oasis.

I like to have the arrangements extending beyond the frame at the top and sides as it helps break up the outline. Flowers don't grow within rigid boundaries in the wild—they grow all over the place—so don't put unnatural constraints on them in your arrangements.

Using some of the longer and thinner materials, cut their stalks to a slightly lesser height so you are beginning to layer the arrangement, and place in front of the wheat and oats. Remember to angle the flowers.

Continue working to the front of the pot, using leafier material to the sides and at the front. A formosa head makes a good central flower to work around.

Push moss in around the rim of the pot to conceal any Oasis. Tie a large bow of raffia or ribbon at the front of the pot.

If you are making an arrangement to match a particular colour scheme, as I did with the triple pot board shown above, it is sometimes easier to coordinate a ribbon than the plants. (To be honest, I've never seen a natural native plant in royal blue. It doesn't mean they don't exist, but I wasn't about to go in search of any. I think the ribbons did the job perfectly.)

Always be prepared with sufficient floral material. It is better to have too much than not enough and end up with a job half done, one that you may never get around to finishing, or one that looks only half done. The excess material can be used elsewhere or made into a smaller arrangement.

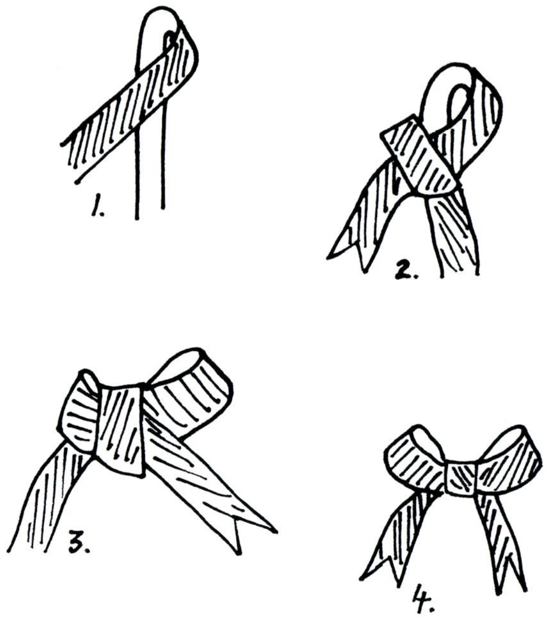

Steps in tying a bow

Roses

Materials

box, basket or pot (papier-mâché boxes are also good—they come in a variety of sizes and shapes)
roses in one or two colours
wheat cut to 25 cm (10") or desired length
lavender
oriental nigella
moss
2 m (2¼ yds) ribbon the depth of the box
floral Oasis
glue gun

Informal arrangement

There is no set pattern for this arrangement. Start by positioning 7 or 8 roses in the Oasis with the tallest ones in the middle; next add the wheat and any greenery, then the nigella.

Complete with the moss around the outside and a ribbon. There are many possibilities here—see the examples on this page and the next for two completely different formal effects.

Informal arrangement of roses and wheat in a terracotta pot

Layered arrangement

Cut the Oasis to fit the box and glue into place. Place the ribbon around the box before beginning the arrangement to avoid the chance of ruining the work by struggling with the bow at the end.

Starting from the back of the box, bunch the wheat into groups of 5 or 6 stalks and push into the Oasis, continuing right across the box. Make another row just in front with the wheat 3–4 cm (1¼"–1½") shorter than the first row. Repeat the process with the lavender, which should be a little shorter than the wheat.

Layer the roses across the front of the lavender in one colour (or alternating colours). The front row of roses should sit right at the rim of the box.

Glue the moss around the rim of the box to conceal any Oasis that might be showing.

OPPOSITE: Informal arrangement of roses set off by a white satin bow and a Lladro figurine

ABOVE: Formal layered arrangement of roses, wheat and lavender

Whole pot arrangements

Materials
pots of your choice
Oasis
glue
scissors
moss
1: Wheat, rice, oats, barley
2: Wheat, sunflowers, South Australian daisies, moss
3: Wheat, lavender, South Australian daisies
4: Wheat, everlastings, South Australian daisies

Wheat, oats and rice blend together naturally with the tin scales and terracotta eggs in arrangement 1

Following the same steps for each pot, cut the Oasis to fit and glue in place.

Cut a bunch of 8–10 stems of wheat (centre flower) approximately 30 cm (12") long. Push firmly into the centre of the Oasis and glue.

Working from the centre outwards, layer the other types of grains, or the flowers, to the rim of the pot, reducing the lengths of the stems by about 8 cm (3") for each layer.

Glue moss around the rim of any pot where the Oasis can still be seen and finish with a raffia bow. For arrangement 1, the grains, I used stem offcuts from the grain to hide the Oasis, cutting them into 2 cm (¾") pieces and gluing them to the Oasis.

Variations

Lavender and roses can be substituted with strawflowers or sunflowers. Tea-tree also works well in these arrangements, but the list of combinations is really endless—see the examples on the next page.

You might choose to use just roses; in this case, do not cut the stems as long as suggested above. You could also have all the roses one height.

For a very classy finish, use a satin ribbon around the pot.

Remember to keep a touch of greenery with roses; this is one way of using up any rose stems with just leaves on.

RIGHT: I placed this arrangement of wheat and dried vegetables in a hexagonal box made from recycled corrugated cardboard

BELOW: The pots in arrangements 2, 3 and 4 are German bell pots

Be adventurous with your floral combinations. You may be pleasantly surprised

Sunflowers

These colourful silk flowers can be used in a multitude of ways. They brighten up any room with their brilliant colour. I have used them in windowsill boxes of differing styles, as topiary trees and as half topiary trees on a board, using two different sizes of flowers. You can also use them as decoration on the rim of a pot, in a wreath or in a garland.

Windowsill boxes

If you are blessed with deep windowsills you could fill a windowbox with sunflowers. You could custom-build a box for the window from balsa or papier-mâché and paint it in an appropriate colour. See opposite page.

Materials
sunflowers (can be purchased as individual heads, with or without stems, or in bunches of varying sizes)
Oasis
moss

The stems of artificial sunflowers are quite strong so you may need pliers to cut through the stems before you arrange them in the Oasis. Use moss to conceal the Oasis. The sunflower stems are pliable so they can be bent if necessary to avoid too rigid an appearance.

For a shallow windowsill a balsa or papier-mâché box could be cut in half lengthwise and sealed off at the back with heavy card or light plywood.

Topiary tree (below)

Materials
pot
Oasis to fit pot
stick
Oasis ball
sunflower heads
moss

Cut the Oasis and glue into the pot or other suitable container. Push a stick into the Oasis

and secure with glue, and cover the exposed Oasis with moss.

Glue the sunflower heads around the Oasis ball and push the ball firmly onto the stick. Remove, add glue to the stick and then fix the head in place again. Tie a raffia bow around the pot if it looks a little bare.

Sunflowers used with cinnamon sticks in a cheerful raffia-based kitchen garland

Topiary board

Materials
board
small sunflowers
2 half pots
Oasis to fit pots
7 cm (2¾") Oasis ball cut in halves
2 sticks
glue
4 leaves
moss

Follow the directions on page 37 to prepare the board and fix the pots to it. Glue the halved Oasis ball and sticks in place on the board before gluing the sunflower heads in place. Finish with leaves and moss.

The frame of the double half topiary arrangement was made from an old maple door and door-frame purchased for $1 at a garage sale. The outer frame was sanded and the rest of the boards were left untouched

Fruit and nut arrangements

Materials
fruit picks and loose artificial fruits of your choice (I have used pears, berries, pomegranates, apples and peaches)
almonds in the shell
moss
half pots
sticks
Oasis
glue
board
ribbon
pliers
glue gun/staple gun

Fruit trees

Prepare the board and fix the pots to it as described on page 37. Once the glue has set fit

The back board for the fruit trees has been scorched with an oxy-torch and brushed with a wire brush for a burned look to match the fire burns on the frame

the Oasis into the pots and glue in place. Push a stick into the Oasis to form the trunk of each tree.

Arrange the fruit picks around the top of the 'trunks' before you fix them in place. Trim the stalks of the picks to the appropriate length with the pliers, spread out the leaves and fix into place over the top of the stick with either a glue gun or a staple gun. Fill in any obvious gaps with the almonds.

Glue moss in place on the Oasis and finish off with a ribbon bow glued to the front of the pot.

Recycled Baltic pine adds charm to this three-dimensional wall arrangement of fruits and sunflowers

The choice of a pot with a grape motif complements the fruit. Some of the very interesting pots now available can be used to great effect

Fruit platter

Arrange the picks on the board until you are satisfied with the design before fixing them into place. The size of the board will determine the size of your platter design.

Add almonds and peaches to the arrangement to make a more tempting picture.

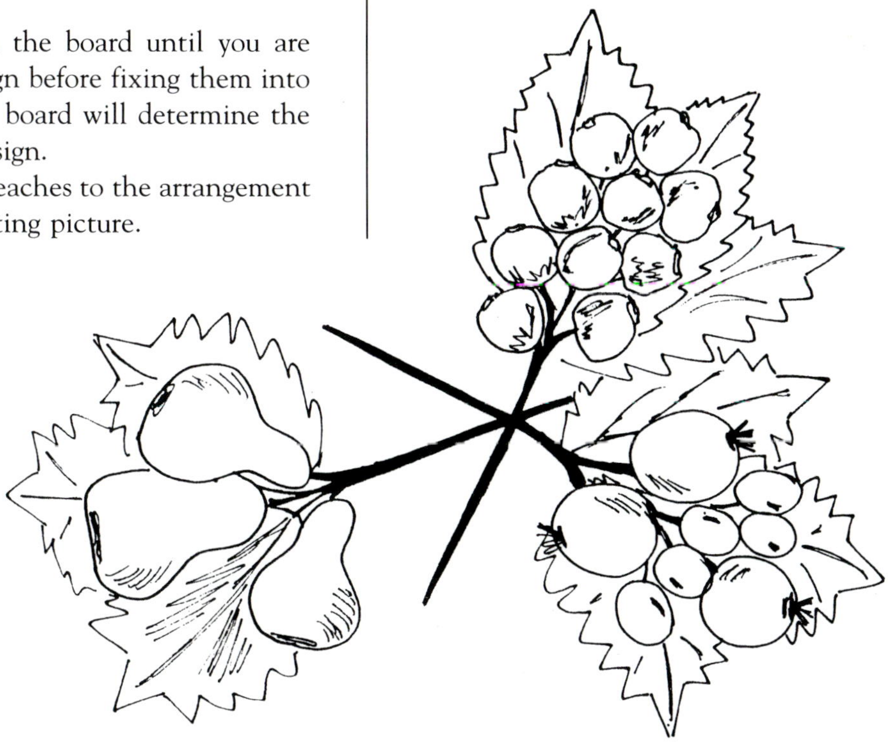

Decorative picture frames

Materials
frame, new or second-hand, any style
print fabric
sheet lace to complement fabric
craft glue
Oasis offcuts
3–4 cm (1¼"–1½") half pot
roses or sunflowers
wheat
oriental nigella, sea lavender or baby's breath

Remove glass from the frame and dispose of it carefully. Cut the fabric the same size as the backing board of the frame and glue it on, smoothing away any wrinkles from the centre outwards.

Cut the lace to the same size and glue on top of the fabric, again smoothing from the centre. Apply the glue generously in the area where the pot will be fixed on so the weight of the pot will not pull the fabric off the frame when you are working on it.

Push the backing piece into the frame and secure with the tabs. Allow to dry thoroughly.

If the frame has no backing, cut one yourself from firm card. Old frames may not have tabs to hold the backing in. Use push-points, available from hardware stores.

Glue the pot in place, following the instructions on page 37. Gently push the Oasis into the pot. Cut the main flower stems to the desired length and push into the Oasis, adding little stems of baby's breath or sea lavender if you like.

Add a bow to the front of the pot to complete the picture. If you use a bi-fold frame, add a favourite photo or print to the other side.

Sunflowers, or a combination of roses and

wheat would look too busy backed with lace and a print fabric. A cream-coloured damask looks very nice as the background for these flowers, and does not distract the eye from the arrangement, especially if you use a large frame.

Variations

Experiment with different types of flowers—do not let yourself be limited by my examples. Never glue an arrangement into place until you are happy with it.

Very small half pots can be glued directly onto the glass or to the frame itself.

The finished arrangement complementing a treasured formal memento

OPPOSITE: Flowers, fabric, lace and half pot to decorate a picture frame

Shadow boxes

Shadow boxes are a very effective way of displaying flowers, favourite keepsakes or a collection of special ornaments.

I found the vintage flower tray on the opposite page in an antique barn. The divisions in this tray are quite large. I have also used sets of old shelves and old drink-bottle crates for shadow boxes. The size of the compartments does not really matter, but remember the bigger the compartment the more flowers will be needed to fill the space. It is a lot easier to buy or recycle a shadow box than to make one!

Although you can use any flowers you choose to fill a division, I prefer strawflowers, South Australian daisies, hydrangea and lavender as they fill an area easily and are not too fiddly.

Small pots filled with roses, daisies, lavender, pussytail or statice can be glued into the box. Cinnamon sticks bundled with raffia, potpourri, oil containers, beeswax candles and terracotta ornaments all look good. Almost anything you have in the house can be used—miniature bears, dolls, thimbles, family photos, needlepoint works, shells, starfish—the list is endless.

On one side of the flower-tray shadow box I have bundled some oats and wheat with raffia and glued them in place. A hook on the other side is a good place to hang any flowers you may be drying, such as lavender and roses, baby's breath from a bouquet or herbs from the garden. A half pot fixed to the side, if the box is wide enough, might make a good storage place for candles.

You might even add a Welcome sign if you are going to display your shadow box where visitors can admire it.

Old oregon shelves recycled as a shadow box

OPPOSITE: This vintage flower tray makes a perfect shadow box with its deep partitions

Roses in half pots

Materials

board of your choice (craftwood, old fence paling, offcuts from timber yards)
half pot
Oasis
glue gun
roses
ribbon
other flowers, e.g. larkspur, sea lavender
filler flowers, e.g. baby's breath, South Australian daisies

Prepare the board and fix the pot to it, following the instructions on page 37. Allow the glue to set.

Cut the Oasis to fit the pot and glue into place.

For any of the arrangements shown here, start at the back of the pot and stagger the roses in height towards the front. Rose leaves are very brittle and break easily, but try to keep some of the greenery with the flowers.

Cut lengths of sea lavender or larkspur and arrange them around the roses as you work. Some pieces might still be added after you have completed the roses.

South Australian daisies can be added once the roses and sea lavender ('Misty Blue') have been arranged across the back and centre of the pot.

Broken-off rose leaves can be glued individually around the roses to add balance.

Give the flowers a light spray with surface sealer to hold their colour in. Finish off the arrangement with a bow if you like.

After a year the roses may begin to look a bit faded and tired. They can be replaced quite easily if they were not glued in place originally.

Roses carry a beauty of their own and are highlighted by the careful choice of complementary flowers in arrangements

Larkspur, roses, South Australian daisies and hydrangea create an eyecatching display

OPPOSITE: Any type of wood can be used for framing. These rose pots are mounted on offcuts that were salvaged from a furniture-maker before they went to the tip or into someone's fireplace

Orange topiary tree

Materials
12 cm (5") terracotta or crushed marble pot
7 cm (2¾") Oasis ball
branch or thick stick
Liquid Nails
secateurs
10 plastic craft oranges
10 almonds in the shell
skewers
bunch of banksia leaf
glue gun
raffia for a bow

Cut Oasis to fit the pot firmly and glue into place with the Liquid Nails. Cut the stick to 30 cm (12") and push into the Oasis. Remove and fix into place with Liquid Nails. Push the Oasis ball onto the head of the stick, then remove it before fixing it with Liquid Nails. Allow to dry thoroughly.

Prepare the oranges and skewers. Cut the skewers into 7 cm (2¾") lengths and use the glue gun to glue a piece into the centre of each orange. You will find the oranges have a hole inside when you remove their centres.

Glue a skewer to the round end of the almonds.

Separate the banksia leaf branches and cut or break into 8 cm (3") lengths.

Starting from the bottom of the Oasis ball and working your way around up to the top, put a dob of glue on the end of each banksia branch and push it into the Oasis ball. Pack the leaf branches fairly closely together so very little Oasis can be seen.

Once the whole ball is covered with leaves, add the oranges and almonds evenly to the arrangement.

Finish off by covering the Oasis in the pot with moss and tying a raffia bow around the pot.

Oranges, almonds and banksia leaf ready to construct the topiary tree

Start at the base of the Oasis ball

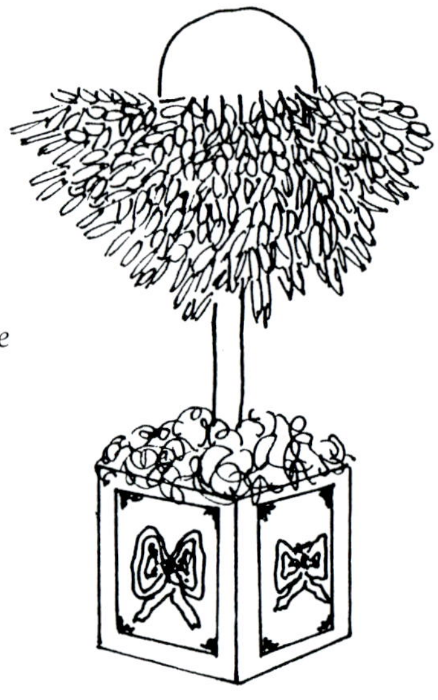

OPPOSITE: The completed topiary tree

Decorating a mirror

Materials
mirror (new or second-hand)
half-pot
Oasis
glue
flowers

You can make your own mirror quite easily if you need one to fit a special spot.

Lengths of picture frame or dado strips can be purchased quite cheaply and cut and fitted together to the size required. Once this is done, take the frame to a glass supplier and have a mirror cut to fit. For safety, reinforce the frame corners with metal corner brackets.

The plywood needed to cover the back of the mirror can be held in place with smaller tabs of ply screwed to the frame (see diagram).

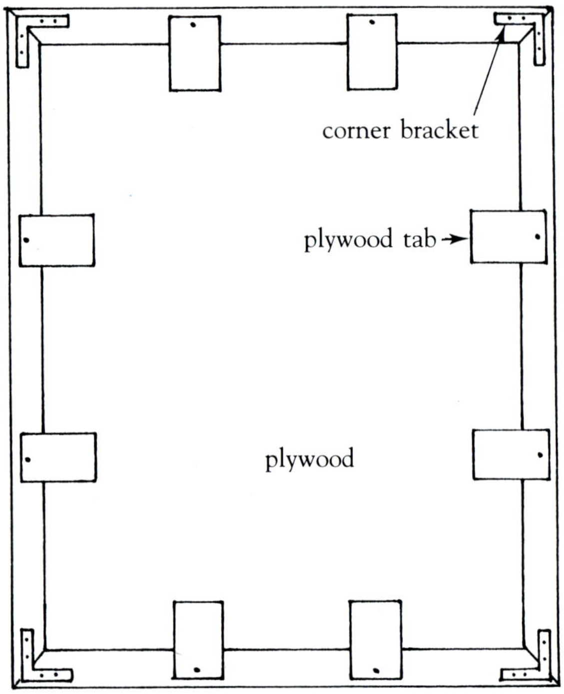

Mirror frame, back view

Antiqued mirror frame with half pot attached to the frame

Once the mirror is complete, position the half pots on the glass or the frame and fix in place following the instructions on page 37.

Fill the pots with Oasis and arrange the flowers in place, keeping the arrangements fairly small and in harmony with the shape of the mirror.

Hang the mirror and leave it for a few days. If you decide against the flower combination you can easily change it.

Experiment with different types of decoration. If pots are not what you want, you can always purchase a stick bundle or a corner-wreath and decorate it to sit on the frame. Another idea is to use a small section of folk-art picket fence to back the pot.

Graduated arrangement leads the eye along the mirror

Christmas gift wreath

Materials
cane or vine wreath
Christmas ribbon
red berries
oddments of flowers
nigella (natural green or sprayed gold)
selection of nuts in the shell
a few cinnamon sticks
bell
small gift ideas (jams, spices, etc.)

Wind the ribbon around the wreath and secure at the top with glue. The start and finish of the ribbon will be hidden behind the bow and the decorations at the top of the wreath.

Glue the greenery on first on top of the ribbon. Next add the nuts and berries. Glue the nigella and other flowers into the gaps around the nuts and berries.

Finally add the bow at the top and the bell. Trim with more berries and/or cinnamon sticks.

In the gaps between the decorations you can add almost anything that can be tied to a wreath or given as a gift. I used small pots of jam, which were secured by a small ball of Blu-tack as well as the ribbon. Don't use glue, for after all you want the receiver of the wreath to be able to remove and use the gifts attached.

Use your imagination with ideas for this very simple gift. Other items that could be attached include chocolates in wrappers, bundles or bags, fancy candles, bath salts, soaps, potpourri, sweet biscuits, a jewellery pouch, a key to something special . . .

Gift wreath to celebrate the festive season

Handy hints

Preparing a backing board

Once a board you have made yourself has been cut to size and the edges sanded, it is a good idea to seal the area where the pot will be fixed to prevent mould forming over extended periods of time. This applies equally to any ready-made boards you purchase, and is especially important if the board is to be hung in a humid or steamy area, such as the kitchen or bathroom, or is made of pine.

If you choose to paint the board for a particular effect, ensure the paint is fully dry before you begin work. Do not try to hurry up the process as you may find you are disappointed with the results.

I like to oil or stain wooden boards to bring out the grain of the wood. Make sure you wipe the boards thoroughly to remove excess oil and stain. Leave the treated boards for a day or two as the smells of oil and stain can be overpowering if not given time to settle. Always work in a well ventilated, well lit area.

Hooks and hanging wires should be attached before fixing the pots onto the boards. This avoids a lot of frustration and the risk of damage to a completed flower arrangement.

Making a frame

Did you hear someone say, 'I'll make it for you' a while back? Are you still waiting? Do it yourself! Making boards and frames is not hard. I am self-taught.

If you are using wood from old fence palings, the rough-sawn look is best. Decide on the width of board needed to accommodate the pot you have chosen. Then decide on the length and mark the cutting line with a pencil and ruler. Two or three panel (paling) widths is generally ample unless you are making something very large. Hold the panels together by nailing two strips of wood across the back, approximately 5 cm (2") from top and bottom, and 3 cm (1¼") in from the sides. Offcuts can be used for this. I use wood glue to hold the supports in place before I nail them, to ensure they are aligned properly. The glue gives added support to the boards and also stops the panels shifting when I am hammering.

A frame around the boards can look good, depending on the type of board and the arrangement to go on it. I tend to use frames on larger oregon boards and on pine tongue-and-groove boards as the edges are not very appealing. The corners of the frames can be made square or mitred at 45°. Either way looks nice. If you do not have a mitre box then square joins are much more easily done.

Cut the frame to fit flush on top of the board, or slightly larger so it overhangs the edge of the board.

Glue the frame corners together and allow the glue to dry before nailing the frame onto the back board. Gluing allows you to check that the frame is square before you fix it to the board. If you have a staple gun you can staple the corners for added strength as well.

To check the frame for squareness you will need a square rule, either fixed or sliding. Place the ruler inside the corners of the frame and adjust the sides until they all meet up with the ruler edges and are flush. To double check, use a tape measure or ruler and measure the diagonals.

Finishing

Boards and frames can sometimes be left as they are, like the frame on page 8 made from recycled

Sandpaper block, tape measure, set square, saws and mitre box are needed to make your own frames

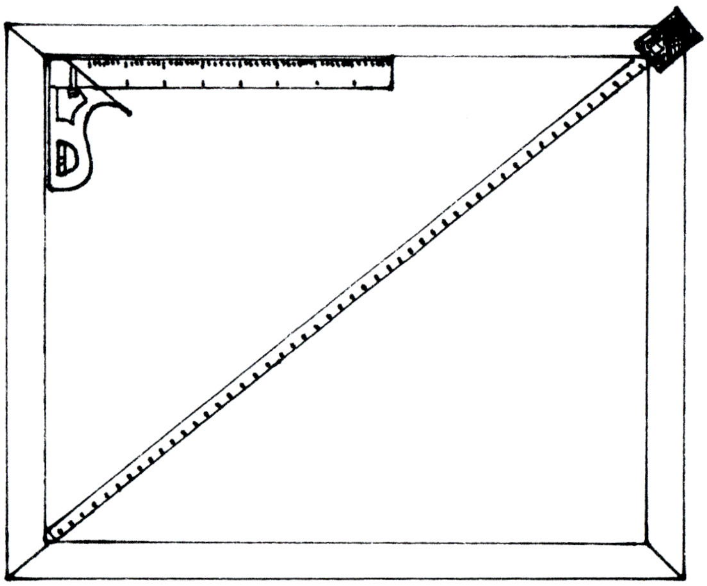

Measuring diagonals to check whether frame is true

Pots and boxes come in a multitude of shapes and sizes to lend character and charm to your arrangements

grey-painted timber; they can be roughly sanded, waxed, oiled or varnished. In general, the more formal the arrangement, the more formal the finish needs to be.

Fixing the pots

It is essential to glue the pots to the prepared boards with a strong fixative. You don't want bumps in the night as pots fall off their boards. (This happened to me once and I was lucky there was no guest in the spare bed at the time!) Use a glue such as Bond-Crete, Liquid Nails or Aquadhere. I don't advise the use of superglue for holding pots to boards.

Always follow the manufacturer's instructions for the glue you are using.

One pot or more?

Experiment with different styles of pots. Try putting together pots of different sizes in the one style, pots of differing styles, pots in twos, threes, fives, or whatever. (Often odd numbers work best.)

Staggering the heights of a number of pots breaks up a boring straight line.

Pots fixed to the outer frame and whole pots set with half pots give added variety to your work. You will need a frame or ledge at least 2 cm (¾") deep for this style.

Boxes

Papier-mâché boxes, whole or cut in half, can be left as they are, or you can glue ribbons on them, cover them in a printed fabric or with découpage paper to create an interesting look.

Other boxes can be made from corrugated cardboard, painted or left plain, or from balsa wood, varnished or painted.

Ideas and drawings

Keep notes, sketches, photographs and other ideas for future designs in a sketchbook or folder. Loose scraps of paper may be thrown out accidentally.

Suppliers

D.M. Designs
Floral kits, completed arrangements, mail order
PO Box 292
Berry NSW 2535

and
7 Bearing Road
Seven Hills NSW 2147
(02) 838-0385

Pottering Around
Queen Street
Berry NSW 2535
(044) 64-2177

Shemara Dried Flowers
Illaroo Road
North Nowra NSW 2541
(044) 46-0078

Native Plants
155 Taren Point Road
Taren Point NSW 2229
(02) 526-1533

Sydney Dried Flower Barn
4 Toorak Avenue
Taren Point NSW 2229
(02) 524-0961

Baldocks Floral & Craft Supplies
63 Queen Street
Adelaide SA 5000
(08) 223-2099

Strathalbyn Dried Flowers
South Australia
(085) 36-3840

C & S Imports
51/55 Seymour Street
Ringwood Vic 3134
(03) 9870-4578